A RIVER OF WORDS

Edited by

Heather Killingray

First published in Great Britain in 1998 by
POETRY NOW
1-2 Wainman Road, Woodston,
Peterborough, PE2 7BU
Telephone (01733) 230746
Fax (01733) 230751

Copyright Contributors 1998

HB ISBN 0 75430 519 8
SB ISBN 0 75430 520 1

FOREWORD

Although we are a nation of poetry writers we are accused of not reading poetry and not buying poetry books: after many years of listening to the incessant gripes of poetry publishers, I can only assume that the books they publish, in general, are books that most people do not want to read.

Poetry should not be obscure, introverted, and as cryptic as a crossword puzzle: it is the poet's duty to reach out and embrace the world.

The world owes the poet nothing and we should not be expected to dig and delve into a rambling discourse searching for some inner meaning.

The reason we write poetry (and almost all of us do) is because we want to communicate: an ideal; an idea; or a specific feeling. Poetry is as essential in communication, as a letter; a radio; a telephone, and the main criteria for selecting the poems in this anthology is very simple: they communicate.

A River Of Words is an inspirational book of verse with an insight into today's modern world.

Each poem within these pages contains verse ranging from the peace and tranquillity of the countryside to the simple pleasures of everyday life.

The poems vary in style and content but all come together to form a talented collection for one and all to read time and time again.

Heather Killingray
Editor

CONTENTS

A Special Puppy	Rita Hardiman	1
Remember	Alf Nicholles	2
Riverhill At Dawn	Martin Beasley	3
Baby	Dorothy McQuillan	4
The Legacy	Michael J Murray	5
Hay Fever	Margaret Ellison	6
The Beggars Opera '98	Leslie Gordon Gray	7
The Return Of The Bricks	Roger Nuttall	8
Music	Margaret Riddell	9
Life	Joanne Cornfield	10
What Might Have Been	Angela Willmott	11
Depression	Shelley Buxey	12
Dear Ellis Peters	Joan Brocklehurst	13
The Last Legend	V Ind	14
It's The Wonder Of Love	Robert Jennings-McCormick	15
February - And The Cowherd's Son	David R Thompson	16
Monet	David Bray	17
True Shaggy Dog Story	Robert D Shooter	18
Hay Fever	Sheila Burnett	19
We Would Like To Believe	Pamela Constantine	20
My Dad	Paul Jay	21
Walking Tall	Elizabeth McIntyre	22
One To Seven	James Leonard Clough	23
Frank	Jessica Wright	24
A Daughter's Plea	Jean Rendell	25
I Cried	Philip Allen	26
Panic Attack	Alex Branthwaite	27
The Falling Snow	Terri Brant	28
I Love Your Summers Derbyshire On The High Trail!	Tom Ritchie	29
Nature	M A English	30
Devil Blues	Lorne Patterson	31
'Eggo' Me	Edward Graham Macfarlane	32
Sunday Tea In Winter	Andrew Mackie	33

Lost Am I	V N King	34
Of Hours And Time	Jeanette Gaffney	35
Excuses, Excuses	Rebecca Crabtree	36
Letter To My Great Granny	Sarah Kaye Martin	37
Under God's Terms	Ty Allbright	38
The Storm	Nancy Scott	39
Dear Dad	Kerry Hibbert	40
Lost Love	Shirley Wynne	41
We're All Missing You Nanna!	Katrina Keen	42
What The World Has Really Missed	Geraldine Moore	43
You've Got To Laugh	R E Sharp	44
Priceless Princess Diana	James Wiseman	45
Football	Denise Fensom	46
Moonchild	David Allan Bretherton	47
Life	Paul Dawson	48
So Very Thankful	Deborah Hall	49
Old Man's Dream	Irene Charlton	50
To Rod	Jill Parish	51
Angela	Penni Nicolson	52
To All Lover's New	Pru James	53
Winter Of The Heart	Joy Margaret Kirk	54
Ode To Heather	D Mason	55
Needs Must	J Metcalfe	56
Love Letter	Cynthia Beaumont	57
Letter To A Childhood Friend	Andy Brelsford	58
Dear Bill	Ron Thomas	59
The Secret	G K Bradbury	60
Letter To A Lover	Patricia Fealey	61
Letter To My Vet	Janice Hewins	62
My Love	Joy Beer	63
Untitled	Brian Scott	64
Hygiene	Catherine M Verity	66
Dear Peter	Jean P McGovern	67
Puppet Show	Marion Schoeberlein	68
The Invitation	Kim Montia	69
A Twisted Mind	R Anderson	70
Special Friends	Elwynne	71

Men And Women	Ria Blackwell	72
The Fox And Hounds	Wendy Watkin	73
Static Time	Fiona Higgins	74
Journey's End	Caroline Gill	75
Words	Colin Allsop	76
Travel On	Phyllis Bowen	77
What's In A Word	Don Okoko	78
A Love Song	David Job	79
Now That I Am Old	Elsie M Corrigan	80
Africa	Coleen Bradshaw	81
The Graveyard	Don Goodwin	82
A Bad Haiku By A Hypocritical Ex-Smoker	Russell Johnson	83
A Cry For Freedom	Johanna Sanderson	84
I Remember That Guy	Mary Woodford	85
Four PM, Beachy Head	Jane MacGregor	86
Teacher Trouble	Dawn Taft	87
Eureka	Betty Pearson	88
Public Enemy	Dave Kwiatkowski	89
Sister, Sister	Saiqah Salim	90
Earth's Stance Alone	Suzanne Doody	91
Memories	D Daniels	92
Untitled	R E Wickes	93
Untitled	Sam King	94
Caged	Michael Morgan	95
The Plague	Deborah Lawrence	96
Checkout	David Ball	97
Train Of Thought	Gordon Knight	98
The Storm Dracula	Annie Doherty	100
Tobias Cat	Clare Davies	101
Gloria	Karen Cook	102
To My Dad	E M Payne	103
Blues In The Night	M Taylor	104
Whitsuntide Sunday	Shirley Cowper	105
My Dearest M	John Coleridge	106
Dear Liam	D G Morgan	108
Dear . . .	Elizabeth Bulleynent	109
Dear Sir	Rosylee Bennett	110

Dear A	Kit Pawson	111
Untitled	Andrew Wickes	112
My Love For You	Susan Kaye	113
Reasoning	D C Wilbrahan	114
Love Will Come To You	Vicki Watson	115
The Secret	J Strathmore	116
Morning	J Dearnaley	117
City Centre Graffiti	R Atkinson	118
Tranquillity	Idwal B Holt	119
His Word	Phoenix Martin	120
Compassion	Alan Compton	121
Love	Jo Young	122
I Miss You Grandad	Sarah Morrison	123
Life By The Ocean	Diana Hauber	124
I Need A Job	Mandy North	125
The Withy Bed	Maïrie Purcell-Herbert	126
My Best Friend	D Wagstaff	127
Wedding Bliss	Carole A Anscombe	128
The Millionaire Beggar	Jocelyn Harvey	129
Tact	R A Southern	130
Dear Tony	Glynis J Cooper	131
My Thanks	F N Forbes	132
To The Prime Minister: The Right Hon T Blair	Drew Michaels	133
Friends Like You	Rosetta Stone	134
Do Not Confront Me . . .	Donald J Butcher	135
A Fan With A Goal	Brenda Whitwam	136
Carers/Caring	M Smith	137
All In A Nurse's Night	Sarah Scrace	138
Care	Jean Paisley	140
Somehow	Shirley Clayden	142
Carers At The Close	Anne Sanderson	143

A SPECIAL PUPPY

A boy went in a pet shop, aged about ten,
He wanted a puppy and saw some in a pen.
A little black and white one caught his shining eyes,
That's the one he wanted, the choice for him was wise.
When he asked how much it was, he was pleased to hear
That he could afford, it, the price wasn't dear.
He told the man he must go home to get the money needed,
His savings had mounted up as some gardens he'd weeded,
The owner said, 'You must be quick or else he might be gone.'
'Oh no,' the youngster answered, 'Not this particular one.'
Within half an hour the lad was back again,
Having paid the asking price, he returned to the pen.
The little one was wriggling and wagging his tail
And squeaking and licking - he just couldn't fail,
The owner said to him, 'You don't want that one,
Choose another from the group - a better one, my son.
He is so very small and has a twisted leg,
He will never run around or sit up and beg.'
But the boy insisted this was his choice,
He was quite happy and wouldn't take advice.
Then he picked him up and cuddled him awhile,
Having fixed a lead on him, he left with a smile,
The pet shop man watched him take the little dog away,
Suddenly he realised why it worked out that way.
The child wore a calliper and slowly limped along,
An energetic puppy would have been quite wrong.
A common understanding, 'You're just right for me.'
Dog and boy united by lack of mobility.

Rita Hardiman

REMEMBER

Thinking back, I recollect,
Though many years ago,
Those bygone days when I was young
And fit, and full of 'go'.

A lad of fourteen, full of life,
By no means lackadaisy.
Impetuous, as I recall.
And, yes, a little crazy.

Climbing stairs three at a time,
And down in just three leaps.
No fear of losing life or limb.
I was here, and here for keeps.

Contented with the simple things.
No hang-ups, spoiled for choice,
A plank across four old pram wheels,
Though crude, was my Rolls Royce.

Careering down the steepest hills
At breakneck speed I'd go.
No need of brakes, with any luck
I'd miss the trees below.

Sixteenth birthday! Whoa, it's time
To pack this childhood in.
Clubs and dancing, girls, romancing,
Shaving both hairs off my chin.

In the street the kids on trolleys,
Reckless, making rubber burn.
Heedless, daring, never caring.
Will those children ever learn?

Alf Nicholles

RIVERHILL AT DAWN

The rush of the water-mill fills the air
The white sun shimmers on the water's surface
One, two, three ducks glide by unconcerned
A sleepy swan nestles in the rushes

This is the place I long to be
Far away from the madding crowd
Where the willow tree is brave and strong
And peace reigns supreme save for morning's song

The swan raises her head from her sleepy dell
(The water rushes interminably on)
And now awake she preens and cleans
Four babies under ample wing
Then nestles back to keep them safe and warm

Can there be a more beautiful scene
That fills the heart with joy and love
O that it could be enjoyed by all
Who are shrouded by man's rude confines

I must say goodbye to this leafy glade
And take my leave of this safe abode
To wander among the runes of life
Farewell for now O perfect world

So let the trumpets triumphant sound
Soar on high o'er hills and vales
And let every spirit be born anew
By the coming of this enchanting morn

Martin Beasley

BABY

The baby plays in his playpen
Shouts for his mother now and then
Just to see her friendly smile
Keeps him going for a while
Soon he'll stand on his own feet
His independency complete

He toddles round the room to see
How mischievous he can be
Can you open this and why
Find out he just has to try
This baby boy is now a son
Cradle days are over and done

Dorothy McQuillan

THE LEGACY

In the slate-grey mists of morning
both sides buried their dead,
and rested.
It was the time just before the leaves
turned green,
and Christ appeared in a dream
alone and forgotten,
and nobody noticed.
Yet, as they watched and waited
through that long dark summer of the smoke,
they hardened their hearts,
remembering.

So tell me;

> Is there a kind of decency awaiting out of sight
> That's beyond the will of patriot or demagogue to fight,
> is there really a leaving of all that's uncouth,
>> A seizing of the hour
>> An embracing of the truth,
> or is the legacy of hatred destined to remain
>> To siphon off tomorrow
>> And spurn a Nation's pain.

> Last night within a dream, I saw the tideless sea
>> And heard the children praying
>> And one of them, was me.

Michael J Murray

HAY FEVER

As I waken, and another day dawns,
I stretch out my legs, and have a yawn,
With a running nose, and a throbbing head,
So I decide, I will stay in bed.

Oh dear!, I'm feeling rather groggy,
Think I'll get up, and feed the moggy,
Have a brew, have a pill,
Rest my head, on the pillow still.

I look in the mirror, and what do I see,
A face looking back, and not like me,
Cough and splutter, blow and wheeze,
As I stifle, yet, another sneeze.

I put the telly on, the weather man says
'The pollen count's high, the weather's dry,'
Itchy nose, itchy eyes, I am sick of all this blowing,
Looking like the red-nosed reindeer, nose aglowing.

Margaret Ellison

THE BEGGARS OPERA '98

The hour is late, and I am old, so let's go back in time,
To when we answered the 'call to arms', the year nineteen thirty nine,
Young and keen, we gave our best, quite often far from home,
Telling ourselves when it was over, that we never again would roam.

Those nights beneath the desert stars, a lull in the fighting at last,
We dreamt of England, home and Mum, of fun in our youthful past,
The 'Desert Rats' they called us, and proud we were of the name,
And after sentry duty we slept, to our record of 'Lily Marlene'.

Lots of those lads did not return, when we lined-up for our demob,
They gave their all, these very brave chaps, and did a first-class job,
So into 'Civvy Street' *we* came, so keen to just start 'living'.
Marriage and children on our minds, all anxious to be giving.

The years rushed by, oh so fast, we lived and laughed a lot,
And when 'redundancy' his me, I didn't go to pot,
Just down to the job centre I toddled, my *'mortgage'* on my mind,
Alas I discover for the first time, goods jobs are hard to find.

They repossessed our lovely home, we wallowed in self-pity,
Forced to move to our present abode, it's a place called
'Cardboard City'
So you who read this please understand, we try but just can't win,
And before you enter your *'hotel'* kind sir, a *coin* for my *'beggar's tin'*.

Leslie Gordon Gray

THE RETURN OF THE BRICKS

The brickworks stood behind my house, it puffed and steamed all day.
The wagons came in empty and took the bricks away.
The hooter blew each lunchtime to let the workers know
That feeding time was over, and back to work they'd go.

The quarry they dug out grew bigger every day,
To feed the raw materials of stones and rock and clay.
One Monday lunch I noticed the hooter didn't sound,
The doors were closed, no lorries came, there was silence all around.

The council came to clear the site. They knocked the buildings down.
Then soon the grass began to grow and rabbits ran around.
I took my dog a walk each day on the site that once made bricks.
She'd chase the birds and butterflies and perform all sorts of tricks.

The years went by, my dog she died. The grass grew thick and long,
Even trees began to grow and birds were full of song.
And then the council men came back, this time they dug deep trenches,
Then laid big pipes and filled them in and closed the site with fences.

They sold the land to build some homes the rabbits are under attack!
It's funny when you think of it, the bricks are coming back.
It's strange, I never really thought I'd live to see the day,
Wagons coming full of bricks, unload, then drive away.

Roger Nuttall

MUSIC

The sound of music wakes my sleeping mind,
Soft cadenzas and brilliant trills.
Filling my heart and brain with great delight
These long ago composers' brilliant notes
Now performed with a magic not dreamed of by them,
Glorious voices raised in wonderful song
Marvellous instruments, string, wind, percussion,
All bent on producing these lovely sounds,
That endlessly perpetuate their wondrous genius

Margaret Riddell

LIFE

As I look through my window
And up to the sky
I think to myself
When will I die.

I look at the ground
At the trees and the flowers
Wondering which one
Has the most powers.

Watching the animals
Run around wild
They almost remind me
Of when I was a child.

Everywhere you look
You'll always see life
Even though it has its ups and downs
You'll always have a taste of strife.

Joanne Cornfield

WHAT MIGHT HAVE BEEN

You touched my heart so deep within.
I can only think what might have been.
You made me laugh and value living.
You filled me up with all your giving.
But I reached out; you were not there.
I need you now, why don't you care?
Something bad happened along the way.
And brought us where we are today.
We've said goodbye and now we've parted.
All I can feel is broken-hearted.
I can't watch as you smile and go.
When there's so much more I need to know.
I long to hold you close again.
To heal my heart, to soothe my pain.
I love you more than words can tell.
But for now my love, just go to hell!

Angela Willmott

DEPRESSION

Depression is navy-blue,
It tastes of liquorice,
Depression is the smell of strong rich wine,
It looks like broken pieces of a heart.
The sound of depression is crystals trickling
through fingers,
It feels sharp and rough,
Depression is upsetting!

Shelley Buxey

DEAR ELLIS PETERS

The chronicles are ended -
You'll write no more of Abbey life
In a country torn by royal strife.

How we loved your brother Cadfael
Gentle Benedictine rare,
Worldly - wise and sympathetic
To the frailties of man.
Nodding by the pillar in Compline
Longing for his spartan bed,
Tending his beloved simples
Herbs for fevers, aches and ills.
Simmering, brewing in his workshop
Syrups, salves and soothing balms.
But shrewd, perceptive, in his sleuthing
When his Abbot sensed a crime,
Tireless in his search for villains,
Staunchest friend to honest men.

So no more tales of Abbey life,
Of battles, sieges, warring strife,
Of a comely monk, in his healthy prime,
Who tended his herbs - and detected crime.

Joan Brocklehurst

THE LAST LEGEND

Gathered, the dust is blown from your cover,
As once again you are taken out to do battle with the intellect.
Your unageing, but wizened face smothered
By time lost memories of countless recollections.
So here we are again my ancient friend,
Draw your sword, gentle your steed,
For time depends upon you again,
As another generation prepares to read.

V Ind

IT'S THE WONDER OF LOVE

It's the wonder of love
When you know at a glance
Your heart starts pounding
And you walk in a trance

It's the wonder of love
When it softens your heart
Proclaiming through life
That you're never to part

It's the wonder of love
When you never shall rue
Not wake in the night
Disbelieving. . . it's true

It's the wonder of love
As you go down the aisle
All the angels are singing
Hearts stop for a while

To the everlasting pleasure
The greatest prize indeed
The wonder of love is glory
Magnificence takes the lead

Robert Jennings-McCormick

FEBRUARY - AND THE COWHERD'S SON

As sheep near their lambing time
And eastern winds hold sway
The shepherd and the cowherd curse
Another phantom spring -
As February winds cut and lance
And lightning lance again.
As trees stand stark -
Awaiting as if petrified,
The next crazy
Crack or break,
Of some demented Sawbones tool
Or Apothecaries - 'Art of wind'.
As gusts in gravitas abate
Awaiting renewed vigour
The cowherd's boy
Takes his promontory seat
He knows he must be able
To watch the milchers pass
And pass again
To parlours
Bathed in storm-clad light
To maidens, hand and pail.
Till all have given up their yield
And none are left a'field
Till a mother's pacing, pacing light
Knows rest
And sees her son,
Come home.

David R Thompson

MONET

His brushwork
left a monument
to art he added
both his precious mind
and heart
his hand
controlled by
both of these
with the gentle
touch of the breeze.

David Bray

TRUE SHAGGY DOG STORY

The school's headmaster phones child's home
on a serious matter so
is doubly annoyed by a rude
reply.
The mother phones school's headmaster
to explain, but is not believed.
Social Worker called in to see
justice
is done! Truth stranger than fiction.
Child's sibs had taught dog and parrot,
when rest
out, to act as answerphone. Dog
would knock ringing 'phone off cradle,
bird would
say, 'Hello, hello,' - Headmaster
would not believe it till shown the
process.
Well, whose a pretty boy now then!

Robert D Shooter

HAY FEVER

(With apologies to John Masefield)

I'm going down to the seas again,
To escape the pollen dust;
Oh, how I long for sea-borne winds
That blow in healing gusts!
For June is here, and I must be
Where there's no hover-mower;
Only the haunting seagull's cry
And white wings over.

I'm going down to the doc's again
To relieve my running nose,
And all I ask is a shower of rain
And some linctus in a dose,
And the windows closed, and curtains drawn,
And the ioniser whirring,
And a bottle of Optrex close at hand
To keep my eyes from hurting.

I'm going off to the chemist's shop
To try to ease the pain,
For every day feels like a week,
And every June's the same . . .
It's at this time that I reflect
That even 'global warming',
In spite of what the experts say,
May yet be good for something!

Sheila Burnett

WE WOULD LIKE TO BELIEVE

Under the sickle-tail moon
The cities of dust arose;
On the tide of flux we chose
Our love's noon.

Perhaps in the dark abyss
That lies between wave and wave,
Between one empire and the next,
Reality makes no grave.

At least, we would like to think,
As we vow our eternities,
That this dark between two worlds
Is not really all there is.

Pamela Constantine

MY DAD

My dad,
Blue pyjamas, smelly, old tatty slippers,
Hairy hands with dark veins and lumpy fingers,
Shiny head, hardly any hair with thin wisps on the top,
Sometimes he is mean, and sometimes he is caring,
He always says 'Night night' before we go to bed,
He doesn't say a lot,
My dad 'Mr Donald Jay'.

Paul Jay (11)

WALKING TALL

There's a big world out there,
For you to explore.
With many temptations,
That are hard to ignore.
Drinking and drugs.
Sunday pubs.
A mess of your life
We don't want you to make.
There will be no turning back
When you make these mistakes,

     Walk away.

Don't listen to the gang,
They want you to join,
In the life of waste and dismay,
They taunt you
With their song,
Never leave you alone.
You will be glad you did

     Walk away.

In the courtroom
They will stand
With God's great book
In their hand.
Telling lies the judge knows is wrong
The old man is dead,
They have made
Their jail bed,
But you won't be there
When they

     Walk away.

Elizabeth McIntyre

ONE TO SEVEN

There is one Mediator between right and wrong,
The Prince of Peace welcomes all in disgrace.
Millions join in the Victor's universal song,
None other love can the whole world embrace.

Romans ordered subjects to carry loads one mile.
Christ claimed co-workers for twice the distance;
When His willing sacrifice shall be our lifestyle,
Then the whole world shall know His assistance.

In this life three great gifts, faith, hope and love abide,
Confusion and hatred's blindness shall end.
May every rebel conscience seek justice worldwide,
Encircling light all despair shall transcend.

Four good neighbours brought a paralytic to Christ,
The roof barrier quickly met its end.
Steadfast prayers are channels of blessing that sufficed,
Faith and freedom giving to every friend.

The lad with five barley loaves, his picnic sharing,
Placed in the hands of earth's bounteous King;
Fed hungry thousands with true pleasures and caring,
Thanks for daily free gifts we gladly sing.

Six days shall you labour and do all honest work,
In homes, schools, hospitals, transport, commerce.
Craftsman Christ from hard constant toil you did not shirk,
To reflect glory through the universe.

Sevenfold Spirit lead us to eternal truth,
Wisdom, Understanding, Counsel, our guide.
Might, Knowledge, Worship, Joy, the inmost shrine of youth,
Break self-concern with goodness glorified.

James Leonard Clough

FRANK

You are such a gentle giant,
And have a big heart too,
That is why Frank Bruno, you are loved,
Through and through and through,

You spread kind thoughts of happiness,
Fulfilling everyone that you meet,
The feeling of contentment,
By shaking hands with those that you greet,

And now you need to think,
On how your life's shaping-up,
I know that when you left the boxing world,
You saw a different life of yours unfurled,

And when you've had time to think,
And of what life can hold in store,
Not only for yourself,
But for that of your family, the ones that you adore,

So good luck Frank with your life,
And with your family too,
May God bless you forever,
In everything that you do.

For the world loves *you!*

Jessica Wright

A Daughter's Plea

Mother you and I have wasted many a year,
But now we need to be near.
As we have shed too many a tear,
Let's loose all those bygone years,
And lay aside all our old and silly fears.
Mother, I need to be part of my family tree,
And have you there just for me.
Oh how I longed for this as a child,
But I always seemed to make you so riled.
I was always the outsider watching as with others you tried,
There were many tears that I dried.
I used to cry why not me to be included?
But my lot in life was always to be excluded.
Life for me was lonely and cold,
But now that I have grown so old,
I have been returned to the family fold.
Mother it's better late than never,
So I don't ever intend to sever,
This new-found love for me,
That has made me as happy as can be.

Jean Rendell

I CRIED

Wrapped
around
your finger
what a waste
of time
My emotions
got the
better of me
and I cried
    I cried
    I cried.

Philip Allen

PANIC ATTACK

Pulse racing
Mouth drying
Panic attack
Falling back

Feelings unreal
Not ideal
Spinning head
Seeing red

Chest holding
Arms folding
Impending doom
Death soon

Fluttering heart
Falling apart
Religious belief
Welcome relief

Alex Branthwaite

THE FALLING SNOW

The snow is falling all around,
Slowly covering all the ground,
Soon it will be really deep,
The sound of footsteps crunching through the snow,
Leaving imprints as they go.

The day is dark skies are grey, but then it is a winter's day,
Our faces frozen from the lashing snow as on our way home we go,
Children playing snowballs, they don't feel the cold,
To watch them playing and having fun makes me feel so old.

Oh, where did my youth go,
As I think back and reminisce,
I used to play in the snow like this,
And build a snowman, and toboggan through the park,
When one is young all these things are such a lark.

But now I am getting old I'll never again be as bold,
I'll just have to be content,
With walking through the snow,
Leaving my imprints as I go,
But I will stop, and wonder now and then,
And wish that I could be young again.

Terri Brant

I LOVE YOUR SUMMERS DERBYSHIRE ON THE HIGH TRAIL!

(On meeting an Australian Ornithologist near Middleton Top)

I love your summers Derbyshire on the High Trail!
Hamlets of stone beside very hill;
Or hidden in valleys among beech and oak,
Elm trees and sycamores,
Where hawthorns provoke!

I come from 'Down Under'
I've seen all the globe,
The Land of Thunder with deserts like the Gobi,
The hills of Cappadocia, full of the bee,
The Arizona Badlands - a beautiful sight to see,
But your Summer's Derbyshire is simply amai-zing to me!

With my glasses I've seen - buntings in the corn,
A tiny goldcrest,
A colt just been born,
The gleam of a trout catching the fly,
The blur of a kingfisher
As it quickly darted by.

Finches and wagtails,
Dippers white rung,
The sight of a blackbird feeding her young,
A lone fox surprised,
A badger at late,
Rare flowers prized, opening a gate.

Cumulus clouds in a quick changing sky,
Watering this land never left dry.
Winter will come, covered with snow,
The hills will look bare, things will just go.
Until the earth circles the faraway sun,
And the swallows come back, when I will return!

Tom Ritchie

NATURE

Nature is wonderful,
It gives us pretty flowers,
Beautiful roses in gardens and bowers,
Dear little daisies peeping in the grass,
Pretty blossom smiles as we pass.

Nature is loving,
After winter it brings us spring,
Tells bluebells their music to ring,
Summer opens rosebuds, buttercups again,
Brings back green grass all over the plain.

Nature is mysterious,
Autumn leaves turn red, yellow, orange and brown,
The wind blows them down,
They dance and flutter in the breeze,
Then make a pretty carpet 'neath the trees.

Nature is beautiful,
Hedgerows are gay with berries bright,
The autumn sun has set alight,
Wild rosehips are shiny and red,
Ruddy haws nestle in their thorny bed.

Nature is majestic,
She rules the world like a queen,
All over the world,
Her beauty can be seen.

M A English

DEVIL BLUES

I went down to the cross-roads, made my midnight plea,
I went down to the cross-roads, made my midnight plea,
Called on the Devil, said, 'I ain't afraid to trade,
Put the mojo in my fingers, and my soul is what I'll pay.'

Gave my years for thirty songs, now my time is gone,
Gave my years for thirty songs, and now my time is gone.
The blues was what I had, but now the blues are dead,
'Cause I can't play no more, what I hear inside my head.

Can't take my pain nowhere, got no refuge in the Lord,
Can't take my pain nowhere, got no refuge in my Lord,
Went and sold my birthright, can't go back on home,
Sent back over Jordan, trav'llin' on my own.

Now the Devil-man is waiting, come to take what's due,
That Devil-man is waiting, come to take His due,
Hope is whiskey and a handgun, a fool's Redemption Day.
O My Lord have mercy, I hear hell-hound on its way.

Lorne Patterson

'EGGO' ME

Edward Graham Macfarlane was the nomen given to me,
By the Reverend John Gilmour of the Auld Kirk in 'muchty.
My Mam and Dad were Christians or they tried to be,
And they planned my birth, (legitimate,) is what they said to me.

My dad had been a 'regular'; in the regiment KOSB
He had served his time in India in the Scottish Infantry,
He had to pay for Barrack Damages caused by his 'boozy mates'.
So he became a *top* teetotaller as his history relates.

He came back here, now a postman, and joined the 'muchty Kirk
He also joined the Postal Union and did secretarial work,
He was Chairman of the Co-op and a life-long *session clerk,*
So with those things for a pattern I was set for 'teaching' work.

I did well in 'muchty Primary, passed my eleven plus,
This was back in 1923 when we did not make a fuss,
About our distance from a school we just 'bore the gree'.
And my place was in *Bell Baxter* a full nine miles for me!

I was in the highest echelon, a *languages course* for me,
with Latin, French, and English, as the way to a degree.
I was brainwashed by my mother's aunt who doted upon me
She was a bedfast cripple with a brain ahead of me.

She made me learn to read the Bible when I was just a lad,
And she made me think about it, which I did not think was bad,
She was really a free-thinker and I can see her now,
Despising men like Sir Walter Scott for his Scottish patriot vow.

For aunty was a *human* with *human world peace* in mind,
she would not let me wave a *union flag* of the *British* kind.
she deplored the *BBC World of Nations* and Anglo kings we see,
She abhorred all inter-nations wars and said,
'One people' we should all be.'

Edward Graham Macfarlane

SUNDAY TEA IN WINTER

Contented cat's purr throbs upon a lap
As crumpets crunch with gulps of steaming tea.
A red-hot coal shifts glowing from a nap
And nervous eyes shoot grate-wards from TV.
Sitting room curtains wrap this cosy time
To hide the frosty ice-pricked lawn outside
Where shivered feathers act out deathly mime
And creatures scratch the rock-hard soil to hide.
The cat alights and with majestic gait
Pads window-bound to take up sentry pose.
The bowl of milk and crumpet scrap will wait
As eyes scan darkness saying 'Halt! Who goes?'
Two worlds divided by a window's sheet
Joined only when a cat and mouse eyes meet.

Andrew Mackie

Lost Am I

Help me find the things I need,
believe me lost am I,
Life has taken leave of me
I wonder why.
Now I have fallen by the way,
life is eating me away
hear my cry,
I wonder why.
Used to hold my head up high,
be a man and never cry
broken now
I wonder why.
They put me in a place away
now my life's in deep decay,
hear my cry,
I wonder why.

V N King

OF HOURS AND TIME

We travel a journey
Of hours and time
With magic and wonder
A lifetime sublime
Where memories linger
As we travel through
And friendships encountered
Are lasting and true
Where loves intermingled
Adventures we've shared
All gathered together
With smiles and care
Ceaselessly moving
This journey through time
The days and the years
Through a lifetime sublime
Not knowing where we will end
How could we know
Of tears and adventures
Ambitions and so
Each day is as new
As the one gone before
We gather them in
As we savour them more
Exciting we challenge
Whatever we do
Each new tomorrow
To find something new
A lifetime of magic
And wonder sublime
Can be found as we travel
A journey through time

Jeanette Gaffney

EXCUSES, EXCUSES

I didn't mean to,
It wasn't my fault,
I left it in the sitting room,
I left it on the bus,
I dropped it down the drain, Miss,
I dropped it in the street,
I didn't mean to, Miss,
It's not at all my fault.
I dropped it in a puddle, Miss,
I dropped it in a river,
It was abducted by aliens,
And so was my brother,
My dog ate it,
The cat was sick,
I didn't mean to, Miss,
It's not at all my fault.

Rebecca Crabtree (11)

LETTER TO MY GREAT GRANNY

Dear great granny, just thought I'd write
though you've been gone almost forty year,
I think we'd have got on famously
though, from your photo you look quite severe.
I've only ever seen one small picture;
In your work clothes, stood in the yard
a wrap-around pinny, long skirt and clogs,
the lot of a farmer's wife must have been hard.
Your grand-daughter named me Sarah,
same as her, and your daughter and mine too;
I've made a scant attempt at our family tree
I'm sure you'd help me sort out who is who.
I wish you could write back and tell me
what you did when you were alive,
I know you worked hard, endured some dark times
got through two world wars and managed to survive.
My gran said you put things off 'til retirement,
by the way, when you see her, say hello,
but you never made sixty, would you change things?
Do all you wanted to sooner, now you know.
Did you greet great-grandad 'Odjy' when he got there?
Were you patient in the twenty year wait?
I remember him fondly, say 'hi' from me,
Did he bring you the local news up to date?
I expect you're busy, with visits from the family,
give my love to my granny, my mum and Uncle Jim, your son.
I'd dearly have liked to know you great granny
but your time was over before mine begun.
I'll close now, your loving great grand-daughter,
hugs and kisses to you, to mum, gran and everyone.

Sarah Kaye Martin

UNDER GOD'S TERMS

If I had four wishes, of how the world should be
the first would be equality for all races, everyone could be free.
The second would be a forceful strictness,
                            yet with the innocence of a child's mind,
everyone could be productive, and yet caring and kind.
The third would be no one taken unfair advantage of,
while working for their special earns,
and everyone loved each other, under God's terms.

Ty Allbright

THE STORM

The shadows deepen, the sky is sullen, grey,
The birds have ceased their melodies, a storm is on the way.

Flowers hide their petaled beauty,
'Neath the swaying trees,
The ancient oak rocks in the wind,
Down come falling leaves.

Nearer and near roars the thunder,
Like a giant running by,
Lightning flashing from the heavens,
Brightening up the sky.

Flashing like a warrior's sword,
In conflict through the night,
Rising to the highest peak,
Then flashing out of sight.

Suddenly the rain comes down,
Enriching the earth by far,
A solitary streak of light appears,
Then an evening star.

All is peaceful, the storm has passed,
Its fury sapped away,
Leaving only serenity,
And tomorrow, a lovely day.

Nancy Scott

DEAR DAD

Dear Dad, why d'you leave us? Why didn't you stay?
What did we do to make you go away?
I'm writing to tell you the price that we pay,
For you packing your bags, and leaving that day.

Mum cries a lot, she really looks rough,
She thinks maybe she wasn't pretty enough,
She tells us 'He's got himself some bit of stuff.'
And that you ran out when things got tough.

She tells us she's fine and she doesn't miss you,
But we know she still loves you and that isn't true,
And you really hurt us 'cos we love you too,
But she says 'Forget him, that's all we can do.'

Why did you do this to people that care?
To people that need you and want you to be there,
There's lots that you'll never be able to share,
Why did you leave us? It just isn't fair.

Kerry Hibbert

LOST LOVE

I lie in wait,
For his call,
The weeks go by,
And nothing at all.

It doesn't seem long since
He came to visit me,
We laughed, we talked,
We walked by the sea.

Life is quiet now, and there
Is pain,
Still I hope one day I will
Love again!

Shirley Wynne

WE'RE ALL MISSING YOU NANNA!

I feel sorry for my grandad
My nanna has not long died
And he's really sad
I know the family is missing
My nanna very much
She had what you would call
A very special touch
She never had a bad word to say
About anyone
And 'Wind beneath my wings'
Was her favourite song
Every night I hear my nanna saying
A special prayer
She's telling God, just let any harm
Come to my family
If you dare
I know she sees everything I do
I know she can hear every word
I say too
But there's one thing I never told you in words, Nanna
And that is
'I love you.'

Katrina Keen

WHAT THE WORLD HAS REALLY MISSED

My dearest Mr Benn,
you should be in Number Ten.
For I want to be a mother
but I do not want to smother
my child to the extent
that she will just resent
my opinions and concerns
until the day she learns
I just wanted to be good
and act as mothers should.
Without meaning to harass
I want her to surpass
the goals that others crave;
never noble, never brave.
I want her to know right
and to fight the good fight,
to see each politician
only worthy of contrition,
to learn to recognise
their bare-faced lies.
Very few can see
we could live in harmony.
What the world has really missed
is a genuine socialist.
Perhaps the resolution
is to have a revolution!
So let's abandon our new phoney
and elect the proper Tony.
Yours truly and sincerely,
from one who holds you dearly.

Geraldine Moore

You've Got To Laugh

You've got to laugh,
You have to smile,
Chase that old sadness
Away for awhile.

Life can be fun,
Hearts must feel free,
Don't give in to old misery.

A day without laughter is wasted;
The best tonic of all is a smile.
'Though sometimes it's hard, it's worth it
You know; you can even make it your *style*.

He's always there,
Wearing a frown,
Old seriousness, hanging around.

So poke out your tongue,
Go, pull a face;
Let the world think
That you're a 'head-case'!

The saddest thing to do is to die
Without ever having 'loosened up'.
No-one in the world lives forever
Go on, drink from your life's precious cup.

For if you laugh
And if you smile,
Fulfilment is yours for all time.

R E Sharp

PRICELESS PRINCESS DIANA

Candle in the wind
Brightly, strongly, burning,
Never going out.
Hearts overflowing,
Tender thoughts remembered.

Beautiful lady, truely inspiring,
Kind and gentle,
Always giving,
Priceless Princess,
Heart of gold.

The touch of an angel,
The smile, the warmth, the laughter,
Softly spoken words,
The eyes of a goddess,
Those adoring eyes.

Expressions of joy, pain, humour,
Feelings from the heart,
Emotions, raw and natural,
So eloquently poised,
Gracious and good,

Eyes flooded in held back tears
True and open love shining through,
Her adorning eyes spoke of her heart,
An inner strength,
Unquenchable.

We cried, we all cried,
Too late we saw,
A true priceless Princess
A gifted God's angel,
Sleep well Diana, sleep well,
We all love you, still.

James Wiseman

FOOTBALL

How d'you convince those who refuse to hear
that it's not all hooligans fighting and beer?
To many supporters it's a way of life
to some, an excuse for a break from the wife.
For release from those everyday stresses and strains
we'll travel long distance in cars, buses or trains.
Caught up in it all, anonymity is found,
to the conformists' ideals we are no longer bound.
The supporters' chants - full of razor-sharp wit,
whatever the occasion, there's a song that'll fit.
Quips shouted out for missed goals and missed passes
or the universally heard 'Oi, ref! Where's your glasses?'
Sometimes it's predictable, sometimes it's a pleasure,
at times, it's the unexpected wins we most treasure.
A chance to meet friends, catch up with some news,
hold your head in your hands, go home with the blues.
No two matches the same, sometimes caught by surprise,
others hardly daring to open your eyes.
Some defeats are harder than others to take -
some games it's more than just pride that's at stake.
It's not 'just a game', it's so much more,
because so many things can depend on 'that score'.
Businessmen, families, all creeds and all races,
the pain or the joy will be shown on their faces.
All this and more together is found
inside the shrine we call - the Football Ground.
So the doubters can sit at home moaning and hissing,
I couldn't care less, they don't know what they're missing.

Denise Fensom

MOONCHILD

Moonchild will you be dancing with the shadows tonight
and skipping across the horizon to escape the daylight.
Will your eyes glisten like the stars arrayed in the naked sky
within the twilight hours will all of your dreams learn to fly.

Moonchild will you be singing like an angel sent from heaven above
dressed in your satin and lace, whispering your verses of love.
Will your heart glow as your lips kiss a fresh breath of air
within the midnight hour will the breeze comb through your hair.

Moonchild will you be thinking about all of the cares of the world
and praying for the children whilst in their beds they lay tightly curled.
Will your spirit be lifted up high as you drift along
within the lonely hours will your compassion build you up strong.

Moonchild will you be sweeping the leaves across the shallow ground
spending some time watching the world spin around.
Will your hands be painting the scenery as you travel upon your way
within the early hours before the sun visits another day.

David Allan Bretherton

LIFE

Walk to the other side of your world
Crawl through the night of silent hell
Your path of destiny has curled
Throw away your dreams in a wishing well

The world turns with a key of survival
Your spirits collide in the mists of time
God speaks between the pages of the bible
Life is a dead end because you didn't read the signs

The promises of life hold a key for death
A mind that wonders back will never come back
Make a silent pray between your every breath
Show us the way but don't give us the track

A key lays inside the cell of everybody's prison
Freedom is something that we have to find
We hear the words but never seem to listen
While the winners run free why are you left behind

Learn each step that life places before you
Staircases of the future will leave you blind
An engravement in diamond of everything you do
Desperately trying to be the one who is kind

A hate builds up for something we used to love
Work hard to the bone just to say the words
A natural feeling of blood ridden hurt
Your soul lives in a cage but you set the birds free

Paul Dawson

So Very Thankful

Sometimes I smile knowing that someone will always love me
Through so much pain and anger, I have so often relied on that love
Sometimes I cry on you for no apparent reason
I keep hoping that tomorrow will be a normal day
Sometimes I hope that peace will some how find me
If I had to stand alone without you, I don't think that I'd get by
Sometimes life's burdens nearly overtake me
I look up and there you are waiting to catch my imminent fall
If I am never what others classify as normal
If my life goes on this confused path forever
If no one else can ever understand me
I find peace in knowing that you will always be my best friend
I find peace in knowing that you will always be standing there with love
I find peace in knowing that you will always be there
                                        with outstretched hands
Sometimes I wonder what I'd ever do without you
For I hate to think if that day was to come
I hate to think of what I would do
Because I am so very thankful for you being you!

Deborah Hall

OLD MAN'S DREAM

The old man sits a-dreaming
Of years that's passed him by
A gentle smile comes to his face
A tear drop fills his eye.
Once he was a soldier, strong and straight and tall
Proud to serve his country when first he got the call
Now his body bent and frail
Hair so grey, face so pale
Wondered where, how or when
Where time's gone he cannot tell
Seems like only yesterday
When he was just a boy
Bouncing on his mother's knee
Filled with pride and joy
But the time just hurries by
That will never cease
Soon he'll find his eventide
To where he'll find his peace.

Irene Charlton

TO ROD

Rod Stewart your record they're playing again
Your music is brilliant, but you are a pain.
'An Audience with Rod' I watched last night
Where you were unkind to a fan which just isn't right.

Sure, your Rod the Mod, your ego I see
But you'd be nothing at all without fans like me.
We can't all be rich and famous like you
But we're people, and you should respect our feelings too.

So next time someone says, say hello to a fan,
Don't knock it, say hi! Be a really nice man,
'Cause it costs nothing, and that's how it's done
And for my part, you'll stay the world's number one.

Jill Parish

ANGELA

Dear daughter, just a line or two,
To let you know the things you do
Are noted gratefully.

Your being there in times of need,
Your helping hand, a friend indeed,
All noted gratefully.

Your tender loving acts are seen,
No words you say are ever mean.
I note them gratefully.

Please remember when you're low,
Just how much I love you so,
Your Mother, gratefully.

Penni Nicolson

To All Lover's New

You meet your love and forget the rest
You've found 'the one', the very best.
Then life seems great, the sex is grand,
But reality soon shows its hand.

The way he flings his smelly socks
The way she discards her crumpled frocks.
She wants to sleep - he wants to play,
He wants to go - she wants to stay.

She says he doesn't pull his weight,
He says the dishes can just wait.
She wants to smoke but he says stop
Sparks start to fly and tempers pop!

And then through bitterness and hurt
Both start to fight and dig the dirt.
Best talk it through and do it now
Before you take that 'Holy vow'.

Try to stop and think what's fair
And choose all angry words with care.
Compromise on life's 'little things'
That way *both* will gain, 'tho *neither* wins.

Pru James

WINTER OF THE HEART

Ask the moon to stop turning the tide,
Ask the sun to stop warming the sea,
Why can't I ask him -
Stop appealing to me,

Stop the summer from falling into autumn
But who can stop nature?
The answer is not important
Instead the sky laughs,
(And the stars) at my tears.
However, in the distance
The last light of hope appears
For when I was with him,
Cupid sent more than a dart
And when I was leaving him,
It was the winter of my heart.

Joy Margaret Kirk

ODE TO HEATHER

I look forward with pleasure to Saturday morn,
My mind drifts away to some imaginary land
In which I am forever close to your heavenly form,
And become the flute, caressed by your hand.

Oh! That I were that flute: being brushed by your lips
To provide a gentle, fluent sound
Which o'er mountain and meadow skips,
And echoes all around.

Thy beauty is never unnoticed,
Nor thy melodious tones,
But thou art observed, as one observes
A golden coin, shining midst the stones.

However, unlike a golden sovereign,
One cannot assess how much thou art worth,
But thou hast the value of the shower of rain,
So vital to our earth.

So if you ever need a friend,
I shall at your shoulder stand -
Your loving, caring, admiring
Fellow-member of the band.

D Mason

NEEDS MUST

One night after working
My hubby the twins and I
All went to the DIY store
Some paint we were to buy.

The twins were running on in front
As the bathrooms we went to see
There to our surprise and in front of our eyes
Was Peter having a 'wee'.

I quickly chastised him and told him
These are not real toilets I said
So I pulled up his pants making sure no one saw
And off somewhere else we all fled.

At the checkout again they had wandered
What a time to disappear
We were stood in the queue, then out of the blue
Shouted Peter so loud and so clear
'Mummy do you remember that toilet?
It wasn't a real one you said
David wanted to 'wee' so I took him you see.'
Both my hubby and I went bright red.

People were laughing and staring
But what is a parent to do
It's not really their fault because their only four
And to them a loo's only a loo.

J Metcalfe

LOVE LETTER

I am looking for you
But you are not here,
If I could be honest enough to admit
Being parted from you
Is something I fear,
How I need your affection
Your laughter and wit.

You hold the cup
That flows over with love,
Gold cannot replace
The things that I miss
So great is our gift from above,
I was born for this moment
How I long for your kiss.

There is little I could not do
Or give up for you,
To be beside you anywhere, anytime
I'll protect and safeguard
This love that is true,
Overcome all fears
Of a dear heart divine.

No love for another
Within my heart strays,
True love is our measure
And blessed our days.

Cynthia Beaumont

LETTER TO A CHILDHOOD FRIEND

Dear friend,

There once was a windmill alone on the hill,
If I close my eyes I can see it there still.
And I think of the summers that you and I spent
And remember the places together, we went
And I realise now just how much you meant
When I think of that windmill alone on the hill.

I remember the brook down in Ten Acre Wood
Surrounded by fox-trots and bluebells in bud
Where we used to go to be alone together
And have our picnics 'midst clover and heather
Where I said 'Don't leave me.'
And you replied 'Never.'
I often remember that brook in the wood.

Do you recall the old scarecrow at Ten Acre Farm?
You used to believe he could keep us from harm
We told him our secrets and innermost fears
He shared in our laughter and shared in our tears
Oh God! How I miss those innocent years
We spent with the scarecrow at Ten Acre Farm.

And remember that snowman we built in the field
On that last fateful day when our futures were sealed
You said you were leaving and I, I just cried
I said I was happy but you know that I lied
And as the snow melted so our friendship died
And so did the snowman we built in the field.

Andy Brelsford

DEAR BILL

Just a note to say we enjoyed the party, and were so surprised
when you said, that when you were young, you was a TED,
and on sixties music you were so happily fed.
Now we've learned to never put a 'mic' in you hand,
for we'll hear for hours every song of every old band in the land.
But you made us all laugh until the following day,
and 'we must have the basics'
you comically repeated in your inimitable way.

But I think of you alone in that little flat,
whether you may be lonely for some company after our lively chat.
You're a jolly soul Bill, and never seem sad,
living by loving, making others glad.
But surely Bill, you have a serious side too.
Although you often say, 'You must have the basics'
perhaps you'll tell me in your next letter, please do.

Your witty jokes we enjoyed,
and they came fast like an express train,
lifting us all out of our pain.
So we want you to know with all of our hearts,
we are your friends bill,
send for us if you're ever lonely, sad or ill.

Our love to you always, from Ron, Diane, family, and Jill.

Ron Thomas

THE SECRET

To him I gave a precious jewel,
Sparkling, rich, new.
Endless hours, searching thoughts:
This gem meant only for you.

To him I gave my priceless gift,
Bravely, honestly, pure.
No longer a secret deep within,
My heart could do no more.

He took it kindly, put it away,
Treasured, safely gained
Within his store of hidden thoughts
His deepest emotions remained.

This treasure shared between us two,
Shining, bright, pure,
Held with love and honesty,
Our lives could give no more.

A secret gem for us alone,
Solid, pure, deep,
Safely held within our souls,
Forbidden love to keep.

G K Bradbury

LETTER TO A LOVER

You used to hold me, I thought the nights
Would never end. I did not want them to.
You always got too hot, then you were too cold,
Crawling into and out of bed like a child.

We made love, tender and beautiful.
You were shy too, but that made me love you more.
The nights are just nights now. I miss you.

Patricia Fealey

LETTER TO MY VET

I murdered my best friend today,
The civilised, hygienic way,
Just lift the phone and you can send
For a hit man, just pretend
No grief, no second thoughts betray.

Give treats to soothe her pain away,
With titbits you fake hope display,
She won't suspect her coming end,
That's how to murder your best friend.

You're doing right my false friends say,
That poor old creature's had her day,
And euthanasia's the trend,
But shame and guilt they will not end,
Because today, this day,
I murdered my best friend.

P.S.
I know that you did all you could really,
And so I remain yours very sincerely.

Janice Hewins

MY LOVE

The sense of loss that surrounded me is slowly fading away
For I know that you are with me, so many times each day,
I see you in the morning in the fox-firelight of dawn
When tiny dew-drops glisten like jewels on the lawn,
You are with me at the window where we so often stood
Gazing at the river and the ever-changing wood,
And when I come home weary, my heart filled with despair
The warmth of our home enfolds me, for I know that you are there.
I see you in the springtime when blossom fills the trees
And in summer's blue and gold days with the drone of honey bees,
When shadows lengthen and autumn leaves begin to fall
And when the crisp, sharp air of winter stills the blackbird's call.
But best of all I marvel and my heart is filled with joy
As I see your face reflected in a fair-haired baby boy.
He little knows the pleasure and the comfort that he gives
For in our little grandson part of you still lives.

Joy Beer

UNTITLED

Faith, Hope and *Love* - these precious things
Are man's unfailing stays in life,
Upholding when the way is rough
And strengthening in times of strife.

The *Faith* that moveth mountains vast
Is comfort when our friendships fail.
With *Faith* in God we can achieve;
Against all foes we must prevail.

The *Faith* that men of old did bless
Is all-embracing to us now.
It cannot fail for God has given
His steadfast and eternal vow.

If man has *Hope* when all seems lost
And none remaineth at his side,
Then he can turn that loss to gain
With *Hope* and God as constant guide.

Faith and *Hope* man's life sustaineth
Through the bitterest of years;
Strengthening throughout the darkness
Of sorrow, and death's mourning tears.

But still, if *Faith* and *Hope* should fail
God's third most precious gift remains.
The *Love* of God can strength afford
And loosen evil's deadly chains.

The *Love* of God made manifest
Upon the Hill of Calvary,
Where Jesus Christ laid down His life
To set His sorrowing people free.

And so, when other things have failed
There comes to us from Heaven above
Faith to strengthen, *Hope* to cheer us
And the greatest gift - *God's Love.*

Brian Scott

HYGIENE

Dear sir,
I am writing to say
How very disgruntled I felt today.
The service provided by one of your staff
Did not make me want to laugh
Oh no, no, certainly not
Never after the treatment I got.
I asked for a cup of black coffee you see
Which was immediately served to me.
Whilst waiting for the coffee to pay
I picked up the milk jug and started to say
'I only require the tiniest drop.'
When afore-mentioned assistant's eyes did pop
'That is not allowed Madam.' she said
'What's not allowed?' I answered with dread
'You mustn't handle the jug of milk
It's not hygienic.' Her tone was not silk.
Everybody was looking at me
Standing at the counter was not comfy
'Forty nine pence.' she said, after ticking me off
I felt so angry I wanted to scoff
'But no,' I said, 'I did not want it now'
I paid fifty pence and took a bow
I hope in future a notice you'll sport
Telling your customers to never resort
To touching the milk jug whatever they do
I am sir,
Yours faithfully,
Mrs Blue.

Catherine M Verity

DEAR PETER

Dear Peter

Just writing this letter to say thank you
For being a friend and a good listener, too
Through the few years past that we have known each other
Through the companionship, we have shared together

Sometimes, a woman needs a man about the house, so they say
Thank you for the little jobs that you have done in your way
You have treated me with such respect, also
Never asking for anything, just food and cups of tea, 'tis so

Thank you also, for taking me out to dine and wine
As long as we know it is just friendship, it is fine
When blowing a kiss across the table, I know it is just foolery
But then, you show so much respect, and good quality

I just must write one thing on paper, you do get hasty
It sometimes baffles my nerves, please take things steadily
Putting things mildly, we all have our faults and defects
We all have our indifference, and surely not perfect

But, I cannot tell you what to do with you life
You are a distant relative to my sister, and I am not your wife
I just wish you would come to terms that Jesus loves you
Because you have the good qualities, this is so true

For our own sake take things easy, and keep yourself well
If ever this letter reaches you, but, for now I bid farewell
Thank you once more for being a good friend
I appreciate the things you have done, as I close this letter to an end.

Jean P McGovern

PUPPET SHOW

Ladies on strings dance,
Men bob their heads showing us
Mirrors of ourselves.

Marion Schoeberlein

THE INVITATION

Bones with black silk draped upon them
Glittering with flies and tears
Bare feet sore from miles of walking
Eyes that speak where no-one hears

Weakened from her stale air diet
Orphaned, lost and so confused
Stands a daughter of Sudan
Who has been shockingly abused

Disease provides accessories for her
She does not wear them well
And death is her persistent suitor
Wants to kiss and then to tell

Her invitation to the famine
One that could not be refused
And yet the hosts have not partaken
Of the fare, themselves excused

Kim Montia

A TWISTED MIND

Stumbling round the circus ring
The children laugh with glee.
Behind the mask a sadness;
A face they never see.

I struggle with my twisted mind
While staring past the gun
Surveying nature's splendour,
The setting of the sun.

A wondrous sight before my eyes
Those hues over lake and fell.
The sky so red and vivid,
Just like the jaws of hell.

My trembling fingers slip the lock,
The barrels empty stare
Two silver bullets in the breech;
The devil do I care.

My broken heart has left me sad
The will to live has gone.
A ray of sunshine touches me;
In life's game I'm a pawn.

To live a lie or crucify
Or watch the sun go down.
In life and death remember me
A sad and lonely clown.

R Anderson

SPECIAL FRIENDS

As we walk our path of life
We meet people every day.
Most are simply met by chance -
God sends special ones our way.
These become our dearest friends
Whose bonds we cannot explain.
The ones who understand us,
Share our hopes, our joys, our pains.
Their warmth contains no boundaries;
So when even far apart,
Their caring still embraces us
With strong bonds felt in the heart.
Their love becomes 'a passage'
Where divisions disappear -
And so these friends God sends us
Are retained for years and years.

Elwynne

MEN AND WOMEN

Things men and women
Do to each other
Walk all over
And lie to one another
Break his heart in every space
Cause her pain in many a place
Emotionally disturb you
Break and hurt you
Causing pleasure
Causing pain
Men and women
We can't connect
Because we are not the same.

Ria Blackwell

THE FOX AND HOUNDS

The riders mount in colourful attire,
Their horses with glossy manes.
A blast of the horn, it all begins,
This cruel grisly game.
Off they go feeling like kings,
To hunt for sheer delight.
Never do they once consider -
The poor animal's plight.

Horses gallop through grassy fields,
Egged on by their masters,
A trembling fox takes to its heels,
Running that much faster.
The hounds go charging for all their worth,
To them it's just a thrill.
Licking their lips anxiously,
Waiting to make their kill.

Horses' hooves pound the ground,
Nostrils flare with steam.
Rising heat from their croup,
Reflects a sweaty gleam.
The fox puts up a courageous battle,
As the hounds search for prey.
Feels his life's in jeopardy,
He sprints and hides away.

Adrenalin flows through every pore,
As he waits with bated breath.
Hearing their ferocious barks -
He knows he's near to death.
When they finally corner him,
His eyes are filled with fright.
But he musters up as much strength as he can
And sprints out of sight.

Wendy Watkin

STATIC TIME

How time stood still when I first saw you
looked upon your face so pure
I drank the sweetness of your smile
breathed the freshness of your eyes

How time stood still that winter day
my heart throbbed in my breast
your heart filled me with joyfulness
summer dawned on a snowbound land

How time stood still when I knew your love
would brighten up my stagnant life
Your love of life shone like the sun
Your tenderness a snowdrop on the lawn

How time stood still on that day long ago
when you loved me as I loved you
now my love is fonder still
while yours is static as once was time

Fiona Higgins

JOURNEY'S END

A golden light came, embraced me and took me to another world,
Free from pain, anger, fear and loneliness,
A light full of love and warmth, such tenderness engulfs me,
I see my loved ones now in the distance, sad-faced and many tears,
Fear not for I am born again in all you do, I am forever near you,
Think of all the good times and smile for I shall remember them too,
Only in time will you realise I have only entered another room,
                                              I am close still,
Be gentle with yourself and remember my love for you lives on,
So think of me kindly and I shall always be there.

Caroline Gill

WORDS

Words of hate and aggravation
Signs outside a railway station.
Posters on a billboard laid
Print on a bill to be paid.
Stories from the start of time
Poetry written in perfect rhyme.
Words of Shakespeare or Lear
Spoken sound all through the year.
Letters on a sportsman's vest
Poetry that rhymes is best.

Colin Allsop

TRAVEL ON

Tho' creaking limbs and eyesight fail
The senses sharpen and prevail
To fill the darkest day with fun
Doing things I've never done
Losing hours in a printed tale.

Roaming continents with ease
Travelling and searching where I please
Sitting in my rocking chair
I travel on

And as I read the printed word
I wander freely as a bird
And go where others fear to tread
Scheming dreaming years ahead
With the printed word I am lured
And travel on.

Phyllis Bowen

WHAT'S IN A WORD

Utterance was He the man up so high
In the vault of heaven above was a word;
                 let there be light
As that was, in the beginning the light.

The light was seen fine the gift of life
It was as good as day and night, and
As the created morning and eventide
In the vault of heaven above was a word.

Dream not of me but that of a word
Birds in the air and the heavens glad
As wasps sing the words of summer wine
What are we on earth without a word?

In my dreams often come my melody of word,
            and the voice of the Almighty Father
                hallowed be thy name, love
To think of a word as an inspiration of love of life.

Believing in the power of a word I am
Eli! why has thou forsaken me?
Indeed a powerful word we all know it was,
As was in the beginning a word.

In words are the sound and music to our ears,
Craven for words to pray for opulence for all,
Our Father in heaven hallowed be thy name,
                    What's in a word?

Don Okoko

A LOVE SONG

You are the gold at my rainbow's end
You are my lover and my friend
My sunshine on a rainy day
The joy that only comes in May.
You are the one that I live for
You are the one that I adore
The colour in the darkest night
The candle that is burning bright.
You are the courage in defeat
You make my shattered life complete
The sparkle in my lonely life
The peace to quench the heat of strife.

David Job

NOW THAT I AM OLD

Now that I am old, think only this of me
When you were small I held you on my knee
I calmed your fears and dried your tears
Would you do this for me!
Would you hold my hand when we cross the street
Now I am not so nimble on my feet.
Would you do this for me, I'm sure you would
When I eat my food and some falls down.
Would you wipe my chin without a frown.
Would *you* take my arm and we walk awhile.
Would you shorten your step to match with mine.
Would you do this for me
I'm sure you would now I am old.

Elsie M Corrigan

AFRICA

Africa is where
The poor people
Live
Without anything to
Give
Such as food, or
Water
Oh what a
Scorcher this country
Is
All of the
Time
How far can they
Climb
With not a
Lot to
Drink in
Sight
With a budget so
Tight

Coleen Bradshaw

THE GRAVEYARD

I chose this plot so you could see
All that does remain of me.
Just some bones and yet I speak
To all who truly does seek
A meaning to the life they live.
This advice I freely give
By the inscription on my stone.
I am speaking to you alone,
What is your foundation my friend?
Is it money that you can spend
Or is your foundation based on fame?
Believe me friend I was just the same,
My foundation was simply greed.
It is the fastest growing seed,
Yet my wealth could not save my life,
Nor could it save my darling wife.
For both of us it is too late,
Because we've passed through the gate.
And once through there's no way back.
Yet Jesus Christ we both did lack,
Now both in torment we do dwell,
God this place is a living hell.

Don Goodwin

A Bad Haiku
By A Hypocritical Ex-Smoker

Cigarettes are an
uncomfortable suit on
a hot sweaty day.

Russell Johnson

A CRY FOR FREEDOM

Under the hot sun we played
Dangling from a tree,
Jabbering and chattering as we swayed,
Nothing could have been as free.

I would listen to the birds,
Squawking in the trees,
Living life like a breeze,
Under a canopy of leaves.

But then devastation
We were ripped apart,
All in a different direction
Loaded into a cart.

The days were hot and humid,
Now they are cold and fresh.
Some people will think I am stupid,
As I run and jump at the mesh.
Surrounding me, keeping me from being free,
Unable to swing from a jungle tree.

The humans come and stare at me
The children laughing, pointing,
Standing, waiting for a reaction to see.

Some stand at my cage,
Tears filling their eyes,
Though I cry too . . . inside.

I try to believe that one day I will be free,
But I know deep down
What will happen to me.
I will die an unknown.
I will die alone.

Johanna Sanderson

I REMEMBER THAT GUY

There once was a Guy who happened to be
A well-known London celebrity
And he was safely locked away
For people to look at every day
But came the time he wasn't there
No more could people stand and stare
Or laugh at him that lovable fella
From London Zoo Guy the gorilla.

Nature gave him a misty brain
So human status he couldn't attain
But from near and far people came to see
His likeness to humanity
But came the time he wasn't there
No more could people stand and stare
Or laugh at him that lovable fella
From London Zoo Guy the gorilla.

Guy Guy is there a place for you
Are you doing all the things gorillas like to do
Climbing up the branches of a leafy tree
Laughing down at all of us . . . in captivity?

Sentimental, yes that's true
To love a great big Guy like you.

Mary Woodford

FOUR PM, BEACHY HEAD
(After the 20th of September, 1994)

The late afternoon sun casts a shining silver path
Which leads over the Channel to where the sky comes down
a straight line to nowhere.
As seen from up here where green land gives way to space
White cliffs above black rocks and blue sea
as seen from the edge, where 12 inches forward
is five hundred foot
down.

Cars leaving the car park and pub drive past
on a road which is set so well back from the edge.
Flip down sun-visors against the golden glare
of Helios and his silver path.
My own way is also straight
and rises with the ground, towards the horizon
straight ahead.
The sea breeze is blowing onto the land, heading
in the opposite direction
to me.

The lands runs out and with four foot left, I stop.
And then run
forward.

Jane MacGregor

Teacher Trouble

Dear Mrs H
I am writing to ask you to please have a heart
You upset my son right from the start.
You yell and you bawl and give him that 'look'
You give him the shakes - (the walls even shook!)
You reap what you sow in life it is said
Just thinking of school fills him with dread.
Your job is so important - you're here to educate
But my son thinks school is something to hate.
So treat him with kindness and soon you will find
That being a teacher is not such a bind
So try and have patience and be extra nice
And all my son's work will be done in a trice.
His schooldays would be good and fun and all that
Then maybe we won't think you're such an old bat!

Yours sincerely,
Mrs T

Dawn Taft

EUREKA

Why can't I grow old gracefully like my tabby cat?
No turkey neck. No wrinkles. No cellulite. No fat.
No flabby limbs. No creaking joints. No failing of the sight.
No need to take a sleeping pill to see her through the night.

She curls up in a patch of sun or on a fresh clean bed,
Sleeps for hours and hours on end, paws beneath her head.
Her body lithe and graceful, young as young can be,
Yet according to *catistics* she's twice as old as me.

I exercise, I watch my weight, do aerobics with a will.
Follow each new diet, swallow each new pill.
Try potions, lotions, gels and creams to keep old age at bay,
And once a week a colourant to cover up the grey.

And what does tabby pussy do to keep herself in nick?
She eats. She sleeps. She stretches. She gives herself a lick,
And sometimes though not often she'll maybe catch a mouse.
But she is very generous, she lets me share her house.

So, just what is the secret unbeknown to man?
Is it the ingredients mixed up inside the can?
Is it the variety? Rabbit, lamb and fish
Smelling so inviting as it tumbles into the dish.

Could be I've solved the mystery. Eureka. It's my diet.
Move over tabby pussy cat, your mother's going to try it.
And what is more I'll have you know my darling feline pet,
Tomorrow morning early, I'm going to see the vet . . .

Betty Pearson

PUBLIC ENEMY

The enemy is AIDS
Who needs it?
A killer-disease
Who feeds it?
AIDS . . . is a public enemy
The world's number one
When will we ever learn?
When it's too late to run?
We must stop sleeping
with people of every kind
having sex with anyone
Are we so foolishly blind?

AIDS . . . the public enemy
is a killer-disease
Why commit suicide
by doing as we please?
Throw away those needles
drug addicts everywhere
Do you really want to die?
Do you really care?
AIDS . . . will one day rule the world
unless we beat it first
until we stop our foolish games
our beautiful world is cursed.

Dave Kwiatkowski

SISTER, SISTER

Sister, sister,
all your man - my man wants is a housewife
not to share their love
But their cleaning.
Sister, sister,
your man - my man travels God's fair earth.
They don't show us
no promised land.
Sister, sister,
your man - my man don't watch the sunrise with us
but show us dirty dishes
and where the 'fairy' is kept.
Sister, sister,
your man - my man wants us to be hidden beauties
in a dust-free house
with the curtains shut.
Sister, sister,
your man - my man are they worth the slave labour?
To cook, to clean,
to polish, to iron.
Sister, sister,
I think it's time to let go of these men
who want me and you sister
to be *housewives!*

Saiqah Salim

EARTH'S STANCE ALONE

Planet Earth, such a miraculous creation,
Humankind threatening it into annihilation.
Such is this beautiful home that both man and beast possess,
What wonderful aromas and sounds upon us it can impress.
So utterly saddening to witness the very Earth one survives on,
Become stained and poisoned,
By that which man defines as technology and of which man
has fashioned.
And now in Earth's fight to survive it remains so alone,
Affecting the delicate balance of life which man cannot condone.

Suzanne Doody

MEMORIES

Memories! The pages of my mind
a book that's held so dear to me
the chapters I'll always find.

> The working days
> The hard at play
> The walking in the countryside
> The long night talks
> The woodland walks
> The meeting of new boyfriend
> The wedding day
> The holidays
> The baby being born.

It's a book that reads of happy days
a book that can't be torn.
This book I carry with me
and read whenever I can.
It's a book that no one else can see
and a book that's always at hand.

D Daniels

UNTITLED

Did you ever drive here, and end up there,
And worry with hindsight having made it?
Can you recall every mile, every windswept hair,
Are you certain that's just how you played it?

What of the man you see in the crowd,
You quicken your pace, your heart missed a beat,
The thought of relating the things of the past,
You do nothing for memory decided to cloud.

It happens to some, it's as odd as a ghost,
Pretending it isn't increases the doubt,
Is there something around recording the most,
Of my life, what I learnt, did it leave something out?

R E Wickes

UNTITLED

He walks down the street,
through the sleeping city.
In the window
a shaman
looks avidly
at the Satan-filled bystander.
Smiling he whispers thrice
a breeze. He jumps.
Their souls combine. One.
I smile as I melt,
self engulfed,
loosing the grasp,
slipping.
Flowing over the pinnacle,
through the forest.
I stop and wait
for the lift.
It doesn't come!
Dissolved I cry.
The green pastures
that once grew plentiful,
had now concealed themselves,
a new layer.
A level past their conception.
Aborted
I laugh
whispering.
As it fades
it grows.

Sam King

CAGED

With eyes glazed I stand and stare
Flashing cameras and remarks keep haunting me
Teasing and taunting with the souvenirs they wear
There must be an answer to all this atrocity

No crime committed we don't deserve this anymore
Listen people to our prayers, answer our plea
Once wild and free, why can't you unlock the door
Animals have their rights, but who holds the key.

For here we are trapped in this permanent show
As I roam around subjected to this confined space
You say it's cruel, but still all stand in a row
As we are sedated each day by the human race

In this solitary confinement proven not guilty
Nothing changes behind these bars each day
How I long for a taste of freedom and sanity
But your thoughts are caged and the key thrown away

Michael Morgan

THE PLAGUE

In 1665, the symptoms came alive
Black lumps and sickness
A sign of wickedness
Those who were tougher
Had longer to suffer
Live in a haze for 40 days
The doctor detected the people infected
Red cross on the door
No friends anymore
Whole families gone
A cure there was none

For over a year
The plague was here
The bodies piled high
More people to die
In mass graves they were buried
Not religious, more hurried
Killed the dogs and the cats
But to blame were black rats

In 1666 came a bit of a fix
The Great London Fire
And its great flames grew higher
The figures are vague
But it didn't kill the Plague
If the story be told
Rats were killed by the cold
The winter came and gone
And the great Plague was done.

Deborah Lawrence

CHECKOUT

Going shopping to Tesco's or Great Mills
If one, unawares, drives
from the old aerodrome on Wyton Hill
down to the ring-road to St Ives

you may be surprised by billows
of horse chestnut and of oak
amid the drifting smoke
of willows along the Ouse.

And you may see separate twos or threes
of geese rising from the glistening furrows
and forming one wide ragged tear
dipping down below the darkening trees
to water meadows hidden there.

And are you troubled, waiting at the checkout tills.

David Ball

TRAIN OF THOUGHT

It looks like rain as I wait for the train, would it surprise you
to say it was late?
There's cursing out loud from the jostling crowd but all you
can do is wait.

We begin the tradition of fighting for position as the train
pulls into the station.
People tread on your feet as you scrap for a seat, whose idea
was privatisation?

We swish and we sway as we move on our way, you'd have thought
the ride would be smoother.
The windows aren't clean on the 8:15 and the floor could do
with a hoover.

Opposite me are a pair of knees and above them a tabloid newspaper.
There's a front page report of an MP who got caught in an
unpolitical caper.

But before I could read any more than I need, the knees turned
the pages around.
What's now facing me? You've guessed it - Page 3! The lady
next to me frowned.

They turn once more and now it's page 4, more gossip and
chit-chat abound.
Before I could see what's not worth a read, the pages again
were turned around.

The thoughts in my mind turn to garden design as I turn and look
out of the window.
You must beg my pardon as I look in the gardens of the houses
that pass us below.

Patio and pond, so quickly are gone as we swish and we sway
our way past.
Quite often you'll find, (and this sticks in my mind) a garden
that's totally grassed.

It'd be easy to keep and really quite cheap to have lawn
from fence to wall.
But thinking it through, apart from the dew there'd be nothing
to look at at all.

I can't say any more 'cause I try to ignore the mess of a garden
that's mine.
And my interest fades almost every day as we near the end of the line.

As my station draws near it's just as I feared - I'm going to get
caught in the rain!
I let out a sigh when I realise I've forgotten my brolly again!

Gordon Knight

THE STORM DRACULA

The storm Dracula casts
His shadowy cloak of cloud
Over the helpless mountain
Cowering, unable to move
Lower and lower he comes
He sinks his biting hailstones
Into his victim's neck
Soon their life blood mingles
And runs free
The mountain is his slave now
It belongs to him.

Annie Doherty

TOBIAS CAT

Tobias was a ginger coloured, large sort of chap,
Jessica was tiny, and cute and compact.
Was it surprising then for people to stare,
As the cat and the mouse made an odd looking pair.
Up the Mall strolled Tobias cat,
Smartly attired in waistcoat and cap.
Proud and erect,
He enjoyed their effect;
While Jessica mouse held fast to his fur
Feeling contented as she heard her friend purr.
The crowds tittered, pointed and gasped
As the two of them journeyed, adjacent, then past.
Buckingham Palace stood magnificent and gated,
Guards standing to attention as they patiently waited.
The Royal Standard fluttered high in the sky
As pigeons swooped low and gave audible cry.
But a great silence fell as the gates opened wide
And the cat and the mouse were motioned inside.
Through chamber and corridor adorned and splendid
Tobias padded silently until the walk ended.
At the end of the room, on her throne sat the Queen,
Majestically crowned and all dressed in cream.
Slowly they approached as the sword was raised,
And then they were knighted and showered with praise.
The mouse gave a curtsey and the cat bowed down low,
But the Queen had a question as they turned to go,
'Pussy Cat Pussy cat where have you been?'
And startled, Tobias awoke from his dream.

Clare Davies

GLORIA

Dear Thief
Head-collar and rope
You knew what to do,
Apple in hand
Click of the tongue
She came to you,
Walking slowly
Towards an
Open gate,
Off the hinges
Now too late,
In a country lane
Out the way
A thief came one day,
Now a hoof print
Her only trace,
In a field
Full of space.

I hope you
Sleep well
Like we do
Now we're alone,
Our friend is lost
Place unknown,
Now we're alone.

Your ever searching friends
Brandy and Jester

Karen Cook

TO MY DAD

When I walk past heather
I think of my dad
The times that we've shared
The fun that we've had.

When I walk past heather
Hear wind stir the trees
The sound of the goldcrest
The rustle of leaves.

When I walk past heather
I breathe in its scent
It's heavy and balmy
It's the good times we've spent.

When I walk past heather
See busying bees
I remember the picnics
The family things.

When I walk past heather
The best things are free
The forest and nature
You gave them to me.

E M Payne

BLUES IN THE NIGHT

One o'clock, two o'clock, will this aching never stop?
Pain all day, now pain at night, surely this cannot be right?
Three o'clock, half-past three, think I'll make a cup of tea.
Kettle on, and tea made strong, all to help the pain along.
When I go back up the hill, think I'll take a sleeping pill
But sure as sure I can foretell, the pain will conquer that as well
The tea is good, no pill compares, I'm very glad I came downstairs
Four o'clock, five o'clock, there's no gain, I think I'll go to bed again.
Upstairs I put on Radio Two, to see if a record will see me through.
At six I feel drowsy, the eyelids close, I feel at last I can get repose.
At seven, my husband, insomnia free, wakes me up with a cup of tea
And just as I thought it was on the wane, there goes that wretched pain
again.

M Taylor

WHITSUNTIDE SUNDAY

We all knew our places,
As we all stood in line,
Five of us girls,
How we did shine.
Hair plaited and new frocks on,
New shoes on our feet,
As we all run off,
Skipping down our street,
Showing off our new clothes,
Was such a great treat.
It was Whitsuntide Sunday,
And we were dressed up to the nines,
As we danced in line.
We wished it would go on forever,
This Whitsuntide day,
But I never thought it would
But it has all gone away.
No more new frocks on,
No more new shoes on our feet,
It has all been replaced with
New clothes every week.

Shirley Cowper

My Dearest M

My Dearest M,

        surely you know not the sure insistent
        cries the hard, bare earth and day-dreams have sent
        across my idle eyes.

        You do not know or haven't sensed them; else, turned
        to me your questioning eyes had surely burned
        with innocent amaze.

        But yet those cries I have most clearly heard
        as if the earth with some sweet soundless word
        had said, 'See life was there.'

        For there among the hedges bare I've seen
        with wondering eyes the subtle changeless green
        and the wild leafy woodland ways which screen
        a sanctuary there.

        In that stillness, dearest M, I'd felt the soul
        of God's creation, unfathomable, whole,
        yet deeply, rarely true.

        And your dear lips and fearless blue, blue eyes
        seemed distant, strange, a transitory prize,
        not that but only you.

        I write, my heart's most precious love, to tell
        you this: Strong, clear and fresh though was the spell
        that swept the day along,

        insistent yet upon the ground I've set
        my step beside your graceful stride. I let
        that greater other song,

that benedicite be gone down other ways.
Our love, your passion, purity and praise
amaze me yet. Only this letter's sent
to confess that momentary thrall meant
Dearest M you are my surest bliss
                                        always J.

John Coleridge

DEAR LIAM

Dear Liam,
Well the way you act
the way you dress
Is that a fact
You sure think you're the best.
People stand and stare
at your long brown hair.
They listen to you sing
but to me you're average really.
You're no big something.

For with the mike you stand alone
think you're a king on his throne
with cocaine to poison your soul.
As your brother seems to fade
no one sees him in the shade
but surely he's the real rock and roll
for you will never find another
quite like your brother,
for he puts the words into your mouth.
So think yourself lucky
for on your own you'd be nothing without a doubt
but it seems to me
that it seems to be
just a joke to you
but when you're down lost in the crowd
without him what will you *do*.

D G Morgan

DEAR...

Don't you know just how it feels
When your love for another is not returned
And yet, your lonely mind still reels
Strange fantasies (unfulfilled)?

And worse than that, seeing them
(Guilty to be jealous but jealous still),
Flirting, smiling, courting others
Torturously close to you?

It seems as though you'll never know:
Sentiment seems not within you;
Nor seems tenderness, affection,
Yet I have so much for you.

I dream of you and wish for you
Through restless night and day,
Yet when you're near, a part of me
Wants you to turn and go away.

Or else, to stay and fancy me
But you don't. Why won't you?

Yours wistfully,
Elizabeth - a teenager with a crush.

Elizabeth Bulleynent

DEAR SIR

Dear Sir,

I am writing this note to convey
That I won't be attending the office today.
I'm running a temp and I'm nursing a cough,
So I think you'll agree I deserve the time off.
In the twenty so years now that you've been my boss,
Tell me - when did you ever take time to discuss
Not once you considered to ask how I feel,
I've come to conclude you've a heart made of steel.

Mondays to Fridays I worked nine to five,
By the end of the week I was barely alive.
If *you* spent a day in the office 'twas rare
It was no use complaining, you just didn't care.
Though you're a grown man, you've not outgrown your pram,
And all of your sentences start with 'I am'.
You spend all your money working out at the gym
To keep you, you say, looking healthy and trim.

If there was a prize for the laziest man,
You'd win it without even raising your hand.
The effects of your 'humour' is wearing quite thin
I only thank God that you haven't a twin.
Yes, twenty so years I've been in your employ
Yet, not one day have I ever had any joy.
So place on the noticeboard under 'Sits-Vac'
'Secretary wanted', for I'm not coming back.

Rosylee Bennett

DEAR A

Dear A,

    Before you
    year by year
    I survived
    my little births, my little deaths,
    my joys, my failures,
    life's fragments
    sufficient -
    or so I thought.

    Yesterday
    it seemed I found you,
    moulding for you alone
    my body of night, my soul of day
    no past, no future
    just you -
    immortalised
    by the moment.

    And now
    you are a memory,
    lasting longer than love,
    your light filters
    through the mist
    that shrouds
    the shadowlands
    where only you and I exist.
                    K.

Kit Pawson

UNTITLED

The more I listen, the less I hear.
What a sound approach, I can't bear them to ear!
The less I hear, the more I dream.
Bold fantasy lie, and silence the scream!
The more I dream, the less I live.
Sweet fiction *allows*, what can worldliness give?
The less I live, the more I exist.
Just as grieving a loss makes one need to feel missed.

As loveless, listless, lifeless souls
Our breath and bodies are filling holes
Where music moves and grief contorts
We silence our songs and live through thoughts.

Andrew Wickes

MY LOVE FOR YOU
(A tribute to June Abbott)

It was dark and I could no longer cry,
My love for you will never die.

I cannot sleep I want to die but all I do is cry.
I miss you so, I miss you more
Please don't go I'm banging on your door.
Please don't go and leave me alone.

We laughed and talked playing in the snow.
Our love together will always grow bigger and bigger
Don't you know I love you so.

It happened so slow I saw you there
Dying but without a care.
Why did you go,
I hate you so.

The clouds came down then it was dawn
The sun came up then it was morn.
I screamed don't go and leave me alone
Know I'm knocking on heaven's door
Begging to be let in.

Susan Kaye

REASONING

The trees still sway in the garden,
Birds resting on branches high,
Spring has brought us colour
How I wish you were here, nearby.

Violets bloom upon the bank,
Primroses gathered around.
Fair in their whiteness daisies flank
Around the pool, just underground.

The timbered seat was meant for two.
But alas! I sit alone.
All the things which we did share
Seems to have turned to stone.

Spring brings thoughts of yesteryear
When the sun was always shining
We think of these we loved so dear
Now in our hearts abiding.

Losing one may be distressing
And we question the reason why?
But spring doth show with all its blessing
There is no last goodbye.

D C Wilbrahan

LOVE WILL COME TO YOU

Never search for love
just open up your mind
whenever you feel lonely
act as though you are blind.

Never sit and ponder
when you are all alone
be optimistic and happy
and cherish your freedom.

Love has such a strange habit
of creeping up on you.
Whenever you feel settled
it'll come right out of the blue.

So never search for love
it will come to you.
Just be patient and wise
and love will surround you too.

Vicki Watson

THE SECRET

Draw back the curtain, let the light fall on me
Where I lie stilled by our loving,
Feeling your sweat upon my body
Spread wide within our communion bed.
I am looking at the flowers you have not given me,
Dreaming the places we do not go,
While within my scalding tears drop blood-red.
As you put on your jacket
You wrap her around your shoulders.
You wash me from your hands
And into your hair you comb
The neatness of your life.
The pattern on the wallpaper is intricate,
Unlike you with your little compartments.
In which one am I? Not that to where you go now.
To a house where a woman is singing,
Unknowing, unweeping, a happy, loveless wife.

J Strathmore

MORNING

As I awake hearing the uproar of traffic,
My heart pounds loudly, my body static,
Children so swift play in the street,
The clump, clump, clump, of running feet.

Bang goes a car door,
The clatter of keys falling to the floor,
There goes the farmer, a blast from his gun,
Shrieking kids all having fun.

Crackle and jangle machines starting up,
Birds flap by as they swoop for a sup,
These are the noises often we hear,
Loud grating harshness that sometimes we fear.

J Dearnaley

CITY CENTRE GRAFFITI

Gripping hard its bed of clay,
Where Brougham streets crinkled cobbles lay.
Exhaust fume black, but bright with graffiti,
The multi-storey leans against the sky.

And it states upon the door of level 3
That 'this is the state of emergency'.
Where Joe-C blazed his name in torn red,
And Mayor and city council seldom tread.

In case the things that they should see displease,
Illusions shattered, leafless concrete trees,
Which under rootless slabs of square cut grime
Spread tendrils out in hopeless pleas for time.
But time is lost for those official eyes,
Which unheard in our social conscience cries,
Was yesterday, and now it has no name,
The tills have rung, and theirs is not the blame.

Now gulls and feral pigeons scrape,
Among the twists of supermarket tape,
That spewed from checkouts, fat and round,
Litter the greasy chip bag ground.
Another majority vote here stands,
Triumphal proof of council plans.

R Atkinson

TRANQUILLITY

I stand on mountain peak,
To view the quilted pattern neath my feet.
Shades of green in undulating waves,
An unexpected treat.

Pine-scented air,
Drifting on a gentle breeze,
Cloaks me in a perfumed cloud,
That makes me feel at ease.

In lazy sweeping circles,
Hawks fly above my head.
Indifferent to my presence,
They have of me no dread.

Clouds sail by, on uncharted sea,
Fluffy cotton ships, on random course.
Ever moving shadows on the green,
From unknown source.

In distance where the sky meets sea,
With soft caressing touch,
And vivid blue and green would blend,
As if by artist's brush.

A panoramic view unfolds,
Of beauty unsurpassed.
I am lifted to the heavens,
I am at peace, at last.

Idwal B Holt

HIS WORD

In the silence of the womb, one voice speaks.
In darkness of the night, one hand guides, sound.
His gentle breath fans even highest peaks,
his loving heartbeat comforts underground.
One staunch embrace gives courage to the weak,
a slight gesture frees prisoners, long bound;
and with his blesséd kiss upon your cheek,
you know you're safe from Satan's feral hounds.
His workings are a mystery to 'man',
though latent 'lessons' *leap* from each new day:
to clarify - where sin our sight had blurred,
to reassure - that when we can't, *He* can,
to chart true course - where anger fogs the way,
that we may heed, through all our trials, *His Word.*

Phoenix Martin

COMPASSION

He sat with her, and listened and listened,
He sat with her but rarely spoke
As the anguish and pain escaped her lips.
He gave her an ear, but no slick answers,
for answers, advice, were not what she needed;
And one felt safe in his patient quiet

Like an anchor in a storm, or a raft in a flood
Was his constant, steadfast presence when depression
Overwhelmed and threatened her hold on life:
Now the storm and the flood and the darkness have gone,
But the vision remains of the one who unstintingly
Gave of himself in selfless care

He didn't have answers, or clever words
He hadn't been trained to collude or beguile,
But he loved, and he cared, and he gave, and he stayed:
It might have been she, but in this case he
Who for richer or poorer, in sickness or health
remained faithful in caring, through love, to life's end.

Alan Compton

LOVE

The first time I met you I knew you were the one.
You took me to the pictures,
We laughed and had lots of fun.
You walked me home, our shadows never parted,
I felt so sure that love had started.
You talked just like a friend,
I didn't want the night to end.
You leaned to kiss me to say goodnight,
My heart did flutter, it felt so right.
You asked me out on another date
I acted so calmly, I couldn't wait.
I lay alone in my bed that night,
Dreaming of my own white knight.

His eyes are so loving, clear and blue,
He's so kind and caring too.
Hand in hand we walked together,
Loving every minute forever and ever.
When he smiles it's so perfect and sweet,
It makes my day every time we meet.
My head's in the clouds, I'm walking on air,
I think we make the perfect pair.

Jo Young

I MISS YOU GRANDAD

My grandad has passed away,
And I've missed him to this day,
I cried and I wept,
From all the tears, I never slept.

I pray for him at night,
And sometimes it gives me a fright -
To think of him at war,
His life that he never bore.

I feel sorry for my mum,
When I look at the medals he won.
I think of what she's feeling,
Surely it all must have a meaning.

Sarah Morrison (12)

LIFE BY THE OCEAN

The soft breeze echoes around the cliffside,
Gentle waves caress the sand,
Sunrays streak over the glowing oceans,
The young and the old enjoy the sun's warmth
against their skin,
Children play happily, without a care in the world,
Seagulls shriek as they chatter excitedly to each other,
Boats bob along the peaceful ocean,
The day draws to an end,
A setting sun,
All life is gone.

Diana Hauber

I NEED A JOB

I need a job
They're hard to find
But what I do
I don't much mind
I've many skills
To put to work
But this waiting kills
I need a perk.

What can I do?
Where can I find
A job for me
That I won't mind?
There's many jobs
There on the market,
There's one for me
I've got to find it!

I'm looking high
I'm looking low
And travelling as far
As I can go.
Someone, somewhere
Can use my skills
So where are you
This waiting kills.

I'll work quite hard
I'll do my best
Please put my skills
To your test.
I'm waiting here
To hear from you
Because I've done
All I can do.

Mandy North

THE WITHY BED

It was the time of year, you see
Springtime. Withy - bed clothed in fresh new green
Would whisper 'Come!'
and this small April child
crowned with celandines
gladly responded, following a little breeze
perfumed with violets,
there cushioned upon a mossy throne
a dreamer of dreams sat dreaming alone.

A child no more, a hundred years -
a hundred miles between, across the void
a long remembered whisper called
and answering, this ageing self-returned
finding no Withy bed,
no fresh green leaves
no mossy throne were to be seen.
Before me spread, in tortured earth
a new floodwater drainage scheme.

Walls of concrete, metal sluice gates,
bare - headed dykes firmly controlling
precisely, disciplined water flow
to who knows where!
Twilight fell, softening, comforting
bringing its own sweet damping.
Through my tears
concrete and metal disappeared.
Faintly, faintly as if from a far eternity
there came a scent of violets.
It was that time of year, you see!

Maïrie Purcell-Herbert

126

MY BEST FRIEND

Dear Cassie as I write this letter,
I hope it finds you, feeling better.
Without your help I could not cope,
So please accept my little note.
You work so hard in all you do,
Looking after me, and Mum too.
At times you do get really mad,
And often you get very sad.
Sometimes you are so good and kind,
Whatever you do you do not mind.
And then things go wrong and I have to say,
Oh what has happened to us today?
I try and try to do what you demand,
There are times I just don't understand.
What has happened to my dear friend,
I try so hard to make amends.
We spend so many hours at night,
Trying to make things turn out right.
Oh why do you hurt my feelings so,
There are times I wish you would go.
And then I think of all you do,
And of all the good times too.
So when things get hard and we fall out,
Let's try and ask, what this is all about.
I want our friendship to go on forever,
So please don't fall out, no not never.

D Wagstaff

WEDDING BLISS

My wedding day has finally arrived
I can't believe that I've survived
Those months of planning so far ahead
Inviting all my friends and family I dread
Good old aunty what's her name
Oh no not uncle he's a pain
I must not leave anybody out
Sometimes I feel in dreadful doubt
Whether I be doing the right thing or not
What the hell I'll invite the lot.

Carole A Anscombe

THE MILLIONAIRE BEGGAR

He has not a friend,
Apart from his money,
But what good is that,
I see nothing funny.

He blocks out the world,
And enters his own,
A make-believe friend
In a world all alone.

He sits in a palace,
Made from his greed,
But who's there to care,
For his every need?

He sometimes wonders,
What happened to life,
The pain of the past,
In his chest like a knife.

Red is his anger,
There's nothing that's redder,
He's nothing at all,
But a 'millionaire beggar'.

He has not a friend,
Apart from his money,
But what good is that,
I see nothing funny!

Jocelyn Harvey (12)

TACT

If I tell the truth, or give the lie
To an uncertain story or tale, then I
Am exiled, 'til such time that I learn
To withhold my views, lest I should earn
The reprisal that comes, when not being tasked
To voice my opinion, without I am asked.

R A Southern

DEAR TONY

Dear Tony,
I hope this letter finds you well,
with time to sit and rest a spell.
I know how busy you have been -
for lots of changes have I seen.
On Irish soil you searched for peace
and helped the bombs and gunfire cease,
but duties here you do not shirk -
you help young mothers back to work.
Now Europe calls for us to share,
I think a referendum's fair,
for that way Tony you can't lose
(if you give us the right to choose).
The only bad thing I have found
concerns the fox and horse and hound.
I do not know how it could be
you did not halt this savagery!
Think of your children, nephews, nieces
chased by hounds and torn to pieces.
See the bloodshed, sit and dwell
on scenes the mother fox knows well.
If on this 'sport' you place a ban
you'll sleep the sleep of blameless man.
Apart from this you've done quite well,
will it continue? Time will tell.
Don't make me live to rue my vote
(I can't stand 'Tories' when they gloat)!
I'll sign off now to catch the post
and go and check the Sunday roast.
I'll have to go - it's almost noon!
Take care . . . and Tony? write back soon.

Regards
Glynis

Glynis J Cooper

MY THANKS

People everywhere in life
From every walk and station,
From every town and city
And every state and nation,
Have given me so many things
Intangible and dear;
I couldn't begin to count them all
Or even make them clear . . .
I only know I owe so much
To people everywhere.
And when I put my thoughts in verse
It's just a way to share
The feelings of a thankful heart,
A heart much like your own,
For nothing that I think or write
Is mine and mine alone.
So if you find some beauty
In any word or line,
It's just 'your soul's reflection'
In harmony with mine.

F N Forbes

TO THE PRIME MINISTER: RIGHT HON T BLAIR

Dear Sir,

People always say that you're fair, therefore I'm writing this letter to you, to bring to your notice a Catch Twenty-Two.

I should get some money because I can't work, (through being ill, not choosing to shirk)! I filled in the forms asking for money but the Man at the Ministry thought it was funny - for stamps on my card alas I have few. So, I am referring this matter to you. The man at the Office said I could have none; no income support, not even a crumb.

Please look once again at the laws and the rules, I voted for you, don't think me a fool.

I am not part of an anarchic new faction, so hope that this plea will provoke a reaction. Please send your reply directly to me.

I therefore remain
Yours faithfully,

Drew Michaels

FRIENDS LIKE YOU

Dear Friends

Such friendships as yours
  make the world a beautiful place
With singleness of heart
  you lessen others' woes
    bringing healing by sharing their sorrows
For the tasks you undertake
  is to remove with its roots - *despair*
    and sow in its place
      seeds of hope

Caretakers to mankind you have become
  and custodians to all,
    dispersed in the land
In the time you spend, giving -
    offering counsel and bestowing love
      you soothe away - *pain*
      and to many hearts bring solace

Services rendered, no return asked
The heavenly signet seals your reward
Friends you are and would be
      whether or not there was a prize
Your hearts abound - *overflow*
    full of compassion

Your loving and giving nature sets you apart
You never pass what your hands can tender
Your words are well chosen, spoken with care
    life you impart - *monumental*
      like apples of gold in settings of silver

Rosetta Stone

DO NOT CONFRONT ME . . .

Do not confront me
with deep furrowed forehead,
cracked wizened cheeks,
once satin smooth,
dull cobwebbed eyes
once sparkling diamonds,
matron's draped figure
succeeding shapely hourglass,
weak croaking voice
from sing-song softness,
rare wisp grey hair,
sparse legacy luxuriant plenty -
all come to pass in loyal love's cause.

So late I comprehend
your heartful, generous gift,
unappreciated, all-consumed,
yet do foresee, hereafter,
hands outstretched shall wave you welcome
into bright Elysian fields,
whilst envious I look on from purging shades.

Donald J Butcher

A FAN WITH A GOAL

Dear Consumer,

Did you join with fellow supporters,
Celebrating World Cup '98!
Did you join in to create the atmosphere,
Though the expense could be a fright!
T-shirts, mugs and collectables;
Novelties in the shape of a ball!
Tissues, serviettes, even tablecloths;
The 'sweet-tooth' needn't worry at all!

Did you unite with the hundreds of fans,
Addicted to the sport!
Did you follow who was *in* or *out*
And able to report!
And finally . . . whoever's won or lost
Will still have a game and a goal;
Knocking out war with all its penalties,
Allowing peace and unity to roll!

Yours faithfully
Denny Rhymer

Brenda Whitwam

CARERS/CARING

So many charities there are today,
I've joined the Marie Curie's Cancer Group.
The leaders are so glad of our efforts
To raise funds to help.
They arrange friendly evening meetings
And fund-raising events - paying for more good treatments.
They are worthy of great praise,
For their loving care and money they raise.
Sadly missed if they were not there.

We as members compose poems for their anthologies!
Helping to raise funds for patients' holidays,
Otherwise they could not afford them.

The TocH president was at the Cornwall fete
Collecting money asking people to contribute.
Gave us leaflets on their good work done.
The PSDA were collecting too for poor sick animals
And the Mental Health Hospital was collecting as well.

All these unsung heroes
Gave their time to these voluntary causes -
Who believe in helping others, not just themselves!

M Smith

ALL IN A NURSE'S NIGHT

Feet don't stop, brain must work - busy, busy, busy, nurse can't shirk.
Bed-pan here, tablet there - busy, busy, 'Nurse, come over here!'
Breakfast time. 'Cornflakes or eggs?' busy, busy, busy,
'Let me butter your bread.'

Water is ready, splish splosh splash, busy, busy, busy, time for a wash.
Doctors come, patients go - busy, busy, busy, the ward must flow.
Admissions in, paperwork done - should we play a trick on Sister,
and have a bit of fun?

Dressings here, temperature up - 'I'll fetch a fan, and keep the
window shut.'
Matron's round, sharp, strict, strong - busy, busy, busy,
'Nurse I think you're wrong.'
Wounds are healing, pain is gone - busy, busy, busy,
nurse is still going strong.

Patients are ill, relatives cry - 'Nurse I want the truth -
is he going to die?'
Consultant's round, doctors thick - busy, busy, busy,
'Nurse, that patient's just been sick.'
Comfort here, empathy there - busy, busy, busy,
kindness nurse cannot share.

Sad scene on the ward, brain-damaged girl died. Nurses all wonder,
were the doctors on her side?
Lights go dark, time for bed - busy, busy, busy, what was it
the doctor said?
Nurse goes home, remembers death's touch - cannot get to sleep,
she cares too much.

Money is spent, wards are closed - busy, busy, busy,
the workload shows.
Cutbacks now, hospitals close - the Government is sorry,
you'll just have to die at home.
Nurse is all alone, no job, no home - busy no more,
what has her devotion shown?

Sarah Scrace

CARE

That little word that means so much
in modern times so bleak,
the people who give people care
deserve to hear us speak.
The value that we place on them
is beyond any wealth,
the way they cope with people who
have lost most of their health.
A cheery smile for some old person
who may be in pain,
helps medicine to do its job and
make them well again.

To sit and listen to someone who
spends time on their own,
makes life a little better for them
makes them less unknown.
So making people part of life and
giving them a place,
what better could you do in life
than see a happy face.

Feeling is a special gift which
really should be cherished,
so many good things have been
watered down until they've perished.

We need our people to take care of
every human facet,
who needs a person snapping round
and acting rather tacit.

Just now the fates are with us and
we have people who care,
who always put their charges first
and in life lets them share.

Jean Paisley

SOMEHOW

(Written for my husband, my carer)

Somehow we speak but don't talk,
We seem to have lost the way.
All the anger, pain and frustration,
We no longer know what to say.

Somehow miles apart I feel closer,
Reassurances over the 'phone.
A voice to light up the darkness,
And make me feel less alone.

Somehow we must find the pathway,
The road which will see us through.
We must stand together united,
ME verses me and you.

Shirley Clayden

CARERS AT THE CLOSE

Amid life's rush and merciless rat-race
Where all ambitions jostle for first place,
There are, through Providence's kind designs,
Rare souls in whom a better spirit shines.

A patient, caring service they provide
And calmly put demands of self aside;
Attentive as they are to others' needs,
Their dedication shows in all their deeds.

And chief among the carers I would hail
Are those who tend and help the old and frail
And who, when human powers are on the wane,
Can bring a smile to brighten up the pain.

They make allowances for awkward ways,
Slow movements and cantankerous days,
Are not put off by insults most unjust,
But still remain quite steadfast in their trust.

There must be times when, underneath their smile,
Their patience wavers, work becomes a trial . . .
But, with their seasoned skill, they keep control,
Not losing sight of what must be their goal.

They know they give stability to those
For whom they care. As anchor in the throes
Of ageing, they are home and family
Escorting them towards eternity.

Anne Sanderson